In the Wind

Catherine Baker

Contents

Explorer Challenge

What happens to the cockerel in the wind?

OXFORD
UNIVERSITY PRESS

Go!

The wind makes lots of things go!

Along

The wind makes things go along.

The man can go along in the wind!

along

Spin

The wind makes things spin.

spin

The mill
can spin
in the wind.

Up

Things can go
up in the wind.

up

The wind can lift things up, up, up!

In the Wind

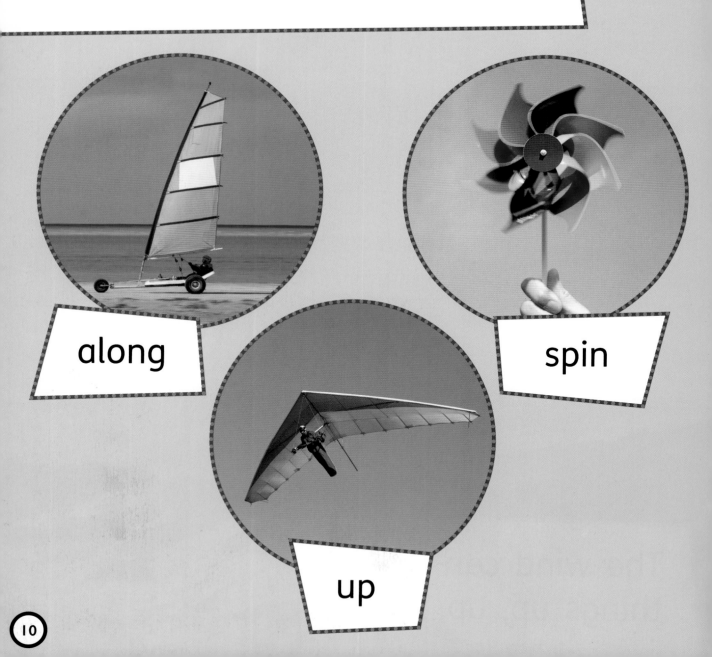

along

spin

up

Look Back, Explorers

Can you point to one thing that can spin in the wind?

Look at page 9. What happens to the paraglider in the wind?

The wind makes lots of things go. Can you think of other words to describe what the things do in the wind?

Did you find out what happens to the cockerel in the wind?

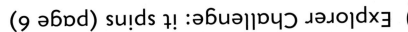

What's Next, Explorers?

Now read about Lin's kite in the wind ...

Kite in the
Wind

Series created by Roderick Hunt and Alex Brychta

OXFORD

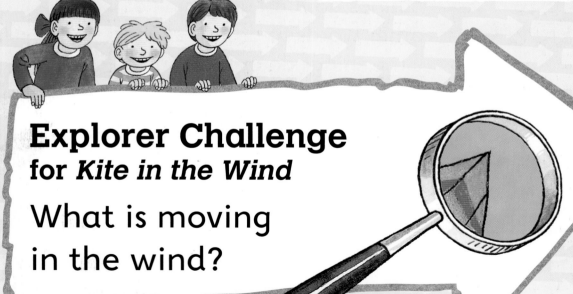

Explorer Challenge
for *Kite in the Wind*

What is moving
in the wind?